Prosperity Is NOT Luck, It's Your Birthright...and Here's Why!

Ruth Fernandez

Contents

ACKNOWLEDGEMENTS

I love you, Jesus.

I want to dedicate this book to my husband, my best friend, the love of my life, Eric, and to my three children, Darian, Nylah, and Shylan. To my mother, Juanita Gallegos, for always being a source of strength, integrity, and stability. To my nine siblings, Jose, Matilde, Lourdes, David, Carlos, Mario, Marco, Janette, and Carolina, for being great teachers and an unconditional support system. To my friends Joanne, Candace, Kimberly, Samantha, Sally, and Vickie who have walked life with me and have loved me through it too. To my amazing team: Jonathan, Tom, and Kevin. Thank you for everything! A special thank you to Erin Funk, who prophesied over me the night we met. She said I would write books. Fast forward five months—my first book! And finally, to Linda Angustain, who prayed over twenty-five years ago for me. Her prayer was: "Above all, I pray you get a revelation of how much the Father loves you."

And I did . . .

BEFORE WE GET STARTED

"Therefore, the promise comes by faith, so that it may be
by grace and may be guaranteed to all Abraham's
offspring - not only to those who are of the law but also to
those who have the faith of Abraham. He is the father of us
all."

Romans 4 v 16 NIV

What if foundational biblical truths were meant to be the benchmark for success in every area of your life?

What if there is a theme and invitation that runs throughout the whole of the scripture that, when radically believed, leads people not only into the understanding of covenantal birthright but also of the grace and promise of prosperity?

What if we could learn to sow the seeds in our hands in the direction we want to go? And what if there was a way to sow for guaranteed results?

Look, when folks hear the word "prosperity" within the Christian church, they tend to shrink themselves into a corner, clinging on to justifiable mindsets that "poor" equals "humble" and "need" must take precedence over "want," especially when putting time in the prayer room of our hearts. Protecting patterns are natural when fear is

5

having a field day, but what if it was never meant to be that way?

Talking about wealth and prosperity in the church can be one of those subjects that tends to get used and abused. Wealth also gets a bad rap with very little practical advice from the pulpit when it comes to our finances and economic growth. On the one hand, there are some who teach that if you just believe hard enough, you can have all the wealth and prosperity you could ever want. Of course, belief and faith are one part of the equation, but there is a lot more to it than that in the economy of the kingdom of God. Then, on the other hand, some preachers try to convince you that being wealthy, successful, and prosperous are things to be avoided—that the poorer you are, the more humble you are and therefore the "closer" to God you become, ultimately leaving grace just for big sin and not big blessings.

You see, in my experience, preachers preach blessing and abundance but usually struggle with the subject of prosperity and wealth. I think this is because it has become a subject surrounded by stigma, and as a result, it has been placed on the shelf of "avoid." Well, in my experience, if we avoid such a huge subject we are actually missing out on some huge blessings, too, and this is why it's actually such an important subject that the faith community needs to get hold of.

I have been thinking about it for a while, and it's why I am here writing this book. It seems that prosperity is associated with prayer for what one "wants," and as a Christian it is better to keep things simple and only pray for what one "needs." This opens a can of worms all by itself because on top of that, many feel most comfortable praying for the needs of others, the needs of the world, and then maybe adding a "PS" of a few little personal requests on the end. I get it—that is loving God, loving one another, and even loving the stranger, and that's the great commission in a nutshell. Having spent years in the church, my observation is that it remains easier for faith folk to petition God for need over asking for what we want, and that's a big subject I want to talk about. There has to be a repentance, which literally means "to turn," from poverty mindsets that mean we are missing a radical experience of God's kingdom, the real-life experience of prosperity.

To keep it very simple, this is what I have learned: If I ask God for what I want, I will never have a need again. Yes, you may want to read that again. If you ask for what you want, you will never have a need again! Can you feel how much that makes your brain sort of squirm a little? Because it is a huge shift in thinking for many and is the most fundamental truth of my story. The GMO (aka genetically modified) gospel calls it greed, but God calls it growth; the religious folk will tell you that it's greed, but God calls it glory. It's truly extravagant and wild!

In John 14 v 13, it says this: "And I will do whatever you ask in my name, so that the Father may be glorified in the Son." It means that heaven engages when I ask for what I want. The Father is glorified, and the Jesus is magnified, and that is the whole point. The spirit of God has been so tangible as I have lived this process, and my prayer is that you will experience the Spirit's guidance too. I truly experience a prosperity gospel in my everyday life now, the words in their purest form, and I am so glad you have chosen to read the stories of my life lessons and what God revealed to me through the process.

Let's Just Call It Out

Before we dive into the fullness of this book, let me share with you how to spot a ministry or minister who has the concept of prosperity and wealth distorted. These observations really are just about awareness and not judgement.

1. When the preacher is the only one experiencing financial freedom and the congregation is struggling physically, spiritually, and financially.

2. When the obligation of tithing and giving is being preached from the pulpit but no education on kingdom financial principles is present in the teaching schedule. That's an unhealthy balance; the more you learn about God's kingdom principles, the more you want to give—not out of fear, but out of faith. Faith is heaven's currency.

Keeping It Real

Seriously, I get it; maybe the mention of "prosperity gospel" triggers you? It certainly triggered my husband and me. For years we struggled with the whole subject of prosperity and wealth and wrestled with God through some very challenging experiences. We did what we were told and checked the boxes to prove it, and when it came to our finances and material wealth we were faithful tithers and givers. However, in a huge plot twist in 2008, we found ourselves in a gut-wrenching situation and lost EVERYTHING we had. We lost our home, cars, my nationwide notary company, and our good credit. It was a critical moment in our faith walk that changed our lives forever.

One night as we were packing to move out of our dream home at the time, I was in my daughter's room sitting on the floor, crying out to God, totally gutted, in pain, frustrated, and very confused. I just couldn't comprehend the situation we found ourselves in, as we had tithed to our home church and lived generously, according to our means. My prayers started with "But God, we were doing it all 'right' " and ended with a holy silence and a pull-on-your-big-girl-pants attitude. I had faith that God would continue to be God and He would just tenderly lead me through this huge learning curve with grace and mercy.

As my sometimes quiet and sometimes gut-wrenching prayer times continued to unfold, I leaned into God in a new way. I was very real and asked questions from what I knew in scripture. I would cry out things like, "The devourer is supposed to be rebuked for my sake, right?!" a truth found in Malachi 3 v 11. In a moment, though, like a shotgun through my spirit, a small little phrase exploded in my spirit that really was like a sword of truth: "God loves a cheerful giver." Such a simple and timely revelation from the Father.

I had one of those "my life flashed before my eyes" moments in a matter of seconds. I realized that we had been tithing out of fear, holy manipulation, and obligation. This revelation was a huge wake-up call full of conviction and was sent to set us free. You see, I believe that spiritual principles must be exercised according to kingdom principles, and the method that God does things by is of a very holy, set-apart order.

At the end of the day (and the beginning, for that matter), God only sees the condition of the heart, and at times we gave and tithed begrudgingly, thinking that it was good enough. The kingdom method, however, is about having the opportunity, with a heart full of gratitude, to be in covenant relationship WITH God and to be a conduit of blessing and abundance on earth. God is not a genie in a bottle waiting to grant our every wish but is a God of righteousness, leading His people in a counter-cultural method of growth and prosperity.

Quick Truth

The condition of the heart at the moment of giving is what carries your seed to the field that it is assigned to.

Cheerful giving is so much sweeter, so much more plentiful, and so much more gratifying to not just your soul but your overall experience of sowing and harvest. The condition of the heart at the moment of giving is what carries your seed to the field that it's assigned to. Dead soil, good soil, or rich soil—our heart's condition is the delivery system of our seed, and this process is the essence of this book.

Finally

No matter what "prosperity gospel" you have heard over the years, I am here to share with you the revelation that God gave me from a young age that has served me well in the highs and lows of being a prosperous woman, wife, mother, friend, business leader, and entrepreneur. I want to bring a revelation that I have never heard preached because, the way I see it, the biblical idea of prosperity is a covenantal birthright. It requires us to be practical and energetic toward the way we do life in the here and now while believing truths rooted in the ancient paths.

I have observed many in the church community stand on the shoreline of faith and pray for miracles to happen to other people when God's love story has always been about the miracle of prosperity, multiplication, wealth, and growth for all who say yes to Him. And yes, every story has its ups and downs, every character has their role to play, but this Spirit-filled story of God is about being cleaved to covenant and powerfully reminded of the promises God made to His people.

I hope that this book changes your mind! I mean, that's a biblical principle right off the bat. *"Be transformed by the renewing of your mind"* (Romans 12 v 2) is both a daily choice and a biological process that takes time. I hope that this book offers you practical resources, an invitation into transformed mindsets, and prosperous outcomes as your faith is radically built up by the power of the Spirit and word.

SO LET ME TELL YOU ABOUT ME

"When Jacob awoke from his sleep, he thought, 'Surely the Lord is in this place, and I was not aware of it.' "

Genesis 28 v 16 NIV

I grew up with a praying mother and a Pentecostal faith in a largely Roman Catholic country in what many would call extreme poverty. We were financially poor; we lived simply, my mother worked hard, and family dynamics were challenging. Honestly, it was a hot mess, and although this book has the makings of a rags-to-riches tale and I will share some of it, the riches came long before wealth, and the rags have revisited me in the form of wrestling with rejection and worth in my journey too. The thing is, though, I had a revelation of what radical faith means in the midst of it all, and it's brought me and my family to where we are today. It's also why I have chosen to write this book. I will be as practical as possible, interweaving biblical principles with real-life examples while offering practical exercises that will challenge your mindset and require some radical honesty. Because, you see, prosperity is a birthright and not a lucky hand.

Growing up in a Pentecostal church, there was always a huge focus on the power of the Holy Spirit and the direct and tangible experience of God's presence. Faith was an experience; it was in my everyday life and went beyond ritual. I radically took Jesus at His word and found myself regularly waiting for the physical to catch up with my internal spiritual reality. For me, prayer looked like something different every day, and it still does. My MO was to decree and declare my way through circumstances and situations, and this spiritual practice never felt foreign to me. Prayer involved targeted intentionality until it manifested.

I have always been one of those people who has prayed until something happens. I would pray until it became clear either to my physical eye or my mind's eye, till it became palpable that God was resonating in and around the thing I was praying for and that a miracle, big or small, was possible and available. I guess that's why I see so much guts and glory in the story of Jacob.

Jacob appears in the biblical narrative a few generations into the covenantal story of God. He had dreams of ladders and revelations of finding God in places he did not know He would be. He struggled with identity and spent a lot of time waiting. He then arrives at a point in his life when he could not go forward and he could not go back. He had to face himself, his God, and his future after a good old wrestle in the dirt. If you have never read Jacob's wrestling story, I suggest you grab a Bible now and have a read. You'll find it in Genesis 32.

What I want to highlight about Jacob is the fact that he started his faith walk surprised by where he found God. He then wrestles with himself, and God and doesn't let go until he is blessed. Jacob did real life: He was wealthy, he had flocks and sons and servants. He was prosperous in so many ways and he still had to wrestle his way to that prosperity. It didn't matter how much economic wealth he had; he had to get his head straight and his relationships in order too. He had to wrestle with God, and his name was changed to Israel by God. "Israel" literally means "one who wrestles with man and God and is able." Jacob/Israel was positioned to fully receive the blessing, and this actually meant sending the son he loved, Joseph, out to the field to seek the *shalom* of his brothers, which had a whole heap of consequences. And so the covenantal story of blessing continued, albeit with some twists and turns.

I have a mentality around challenges that if I have to, I will wrestle it down in the presence of God until something happens. I decree and declare and I use what is in my hands. I am generous and I ask for what I want as well as what I need. I take God radically at His word. It's a very effective method for me, and I do it with everything. I have learned that you cannot have radical faith without boldness. I pray in this way around physical, spiritual, and financial matters, with my health, my brokenness, and my fears. It's real life and although I drive my kids crazy, I pray that they will testify one day that they, too, grew up with a praying mother who prayed bold prayers and saw God move, provide, and multiply all we had been given in powerful ways.

CHAPTER 1 – The Power of Prosperity

"This is what we speak, not in words taught us by human wisdom but in words taught by the Spirit, explaining spiritual realities with Spirit-taught words."

1 Corinthians 2 v 13

As someone who devours books, I am always fascinated by language and how words are defined, used, and sometimes commonly understood. If there is a word that has caused confusion, intrigue, or seems to cause other people problems, I like to know what we are really talking about. This has never been truer than with the word "PROSPERITY."

Here is a mishmash of definitions for the word "prosperity" that I gathered from Webster's dictionary as well as gleaning some understandings from the Greek and Hebrew meanings. We have to start this conversation with establishing what this bold word means.

Prosperity:

The condition of being SUCCESSFUL or THRIVING.

To become STRONG and FLOURISHING.

PLENTY.

To be OVER and ABOVE, to ABOUND.

ADVANCE or GAIN in anything GOOD or DESIRABLE.

DELIVERANCE. SALVATION.

PEACE, SHALOM, WHOLENESS.

MORE than ENOUGH.

PROGRESS in business or enterprise.

COMPLETENESS and SOUNDNESS.

What a foundational, faith-building word! As you can see, prosperity is not all about money. Prosperity consists of so much more than that. It's a comprehensive, all-encompassing variety of good things for your life, finances included.

Right off the bat I want you to know that prosperity is not something that you earn. You don't have to be perfect; you don't have to be all those things that the corporate church tells you that you should be. You have just got to navigate the tension of digging in your heels while walking in obedience. You may, as you read this book, find yourself looking at your life, saying, "I have wasted so much time," but I need you to hear this loud and clear: You can do this now! Nothing is lost—grace is both grit and guts, and your future will look different.

As you read this book, I want you to remember these definitions of prosperity. Circle the words that stand out to you in the definition, write them in your journal, and use them to steady your feet on the path ahead. It's time to see prosperity and wealth in a new way.

Dig in Your Heels

Grab a notebook and start making a few notes around the following questions. It's going to be important to journal as much as you can as you read this book. There will be a number of exercises for you to participate in.

Why have you chosen to read this book?

What are you intentionally offering to God as you say yes to the subjects of wealth and prosperity?

Do you hold a bias or stigma when it comes to talking about wealth and prosperity?

Have you ever been challenged to think differently about your finances and wealth?

Have you ever been invited to get your hands in the mud and evaluate your finances with radical honesty?

However you have answered the above questions, maybe you are reading this book because, quite simply, you want things to change. You may be feeling a fire in your belly even now as you step out to choose radical, heaven-shaking faith to engage with the promises of God's covenant blessings for you, your family, and the generations that will follow.

At the end of each chapter I will offer you some declarations, decrees, and scriptures to speak out loud. You can return to them at any point and use them to help transform your mind and declare freedom. This book is going to be a practical, whole-being experience, so brace yourself for the work, don't get distracted, and enjoy the ride, 'cause we've got work to do!

Breakthrough Declarations and Decrees – Prosperity

I renounce all lies, false teachings, and anti-prosperity spirits seeking to keep me exempt from your plan to prosper me.

I renounce all fear connected to success and demons that would seek to deceive me from walking in my inheritance of prosperity concerning natural and spiritual things.

I decree cheerful giving is my portion. I'm loosed from all resentful giving and giving out of necessity.

I renounce every vow and pledge to poverty rooted in religious error, ignorance, and bloodline issues in Jesus's name!

I decree that as I obey the Lord and serve Him, I'll spend my days in prosperity and years in pleasure according to Job 36 v 11.

Beloved, I pray that in all respects you may prosper and be in good health, just as your soul prospers. (3 John 2)

CHAPTER 2 – The Power of Covenant Revelation

"I will establish my covenant between me and you and your descendants after you throughout their generations as an everlasting covenant, to be God to you and to your descendants after you."

Genesis 17 v 7 (NASB)

"He redeemed us in order that the blessing given to Abraham might come to the Gentiles through Christ Jesus, so that by faith we might receive the promise of the Spirit."

Galatians 3 v 14 (NIV)

The revelation that God gave me in my own life about the power of covenant has made more and more sense the older I have gotten. The prophetic promises and experiences within my story, the big prayers prayed, the times of loss, and the times of prosperity were rooted in God's covenant before I was even fully conscious of it, and that's the point. The covenant made by God to His people is a promise made by Him to establish His kingdom on the earth. The promises are established before our "YES," and they remain always true whether we believe them or not. It is by faith through Jesus and in the receiving of the Spirit that we get to walk in the everlasting covenant that God established for all generations.

The Abrahamic Covenant is an unconditional covenant, and the story starts in Genesis 12 v 1–3.

"The Lord had said to Abram, 'Go from your country, your people, and your father's household to the land I will show you. I will make you into a great nation, and I will bless you; I will make your name great, and you will be a blessing. I will bless those who bless you, and whoever curses you, I will curse; and all peoples on earth will be blessed through you."

Genesis 12 v 1–3 NIV

God makes things pretty clear that His covenant was about the radical power of expansion, from a land that he would come to see (Genesis 13 v 14) to the expansion and change in the name of both Abraham and his wife, Sarah. God changed Abraham's name from Abram ("high father") to Abraham ("father of a multitude"). I have heard that it is the H added to Abraham's name that is a picture of God's name, Yahweh, being added. The picture of the breath of God being added not only fulfilled a promise from the covenant in the enlargement of his name but also was a prophetic sign for Abraham's capacity for faith-filled prosperity.

There is a ceremony then recorded in Genesis 15 that indicates the unconditional nature of the covenant. God clearly defines what the future will hold—the good, the bad, and the ugly—while also establishing the land He was promising the descendants of Abraham. In ancient times, when a covenant was dependent upon both parties keeping commitments, both would pass between the pieces of animals. In Genesis 15, God alone moves between the halves of the animals. In fact, Abraham was in a deep sleep at the time. God's solitary action indicates that the covenant is principally His promise. He binds Himself to the covenant, maybe knowing just how hard it would be for humanity to believe and have the kind of faith that was required to receive all He had for them . . . for us.

Quick Truth

God establishing His covenant on the earth was about the radical power of expansion.

The Sign of the Covenant, Two Sons, and a Test

Later, God gave Abraham the act of circumcision as the specific sign of the Abrahamic covenant (Genesis 17 v 9–14). All males in Abraham's line were to be circumcised and carry with them a lifelong mark in their flesh that they were part of God's physical blessing in the world. As the biblical text repeats over and over again, the Abrahamic covenant is unconditional. It should also be taken literally. There is no need to over spiritualize the promise to Abraham. God's promises to Abraham's descendants would be fulfilled literally.

One of the defining moments of the covenant established in Abraham and Sarah's life was their long conversation with God about being childless. I mean, it doesn't get any more challenging than being promised descendants that number the stars without a child of their own. They make choices along the way to "fix" the situation and Abraham ends up with a son from Sarah's maidservant, Hagar. Ishmael was born and would go on to inherit some of his father's wealth, but he would never receive the covenant blessings that were established by God with Abraham and Sarah. God was very specific that the covenant would be through their union. God had a plan and despite the many ups and downs, Abraham kept on walking by faith.

Abraham and Sarah go on to have a son called Isaac, and when Isaac is in his early teens, God tests Abraham in a way that makes my momma heart take a really deep breath. God told him, *"Take your son, your only son, Isaac, whom you love and go to the land of Moriah and offer him there as a burnt offering on one of the mountains of which I shall tell you"* (Genesis 22 v 2). "Moriah" in biblical Hebrew means "God is my teacher," so we can only assume that there would be a lesson to be learned. All this being said, it would have been a tremendous shock to any parent to be blessed by a long-awaited child, only to have God tell you to sacrifice that child.

The Bible does not say that Abraham hesitated for a moment. In fact, there are certain passages that indicate Abraham's strong faith that God would not take his son at all (Genesis 22 v 5, 8). Abraham believed that God would raise Isaac back to life if the sacrifice actually did take place (Hebrews 11 v 19). Whether for God's, Abraham's, Isaac's, or for our sake as an example, Abraham took his son up the mountain, laid him down, and prepared to kill him in obedience to God's command. However, God intervened by stopping Abraham from killing his son and by providing a sacrifice in the form of a ram caught in the nearby brush. While Abraham's faith had been tested, he proved his faith by his obedience to God. In the picture of a ram being provided, a male father sheep, I can't help but think that this substitute was more about making room for the covenant blessing to be passed to the next generation, to Isaac, and what it meant for him to witness the faith of his father and the faithfulness of God.

The Father of Faith

Abraham had a long and challenging journey and he worked hard, experiencing grief and blessings. Most of the time, he wasn't able to see the path ahead, but he held strong to the promise in his heart. God would continue to fulfill that promise over a thousand years after Abraham's death until its completion in His Son Jesus. We know through Abraham that God always keeps His promises. We may not have all the answers, but God surely does.

The Lord promised to bless Abraham and make him the father of many nations. He promised to make him exceedingly fruitful, to keep His covenant with him throughout the generations, and to give his descendants the land He showed him for an everlasting possession (Genesis 17 v 4-8). In Genesis 22 v 17, the Lord told Abraham that "In blessing I will bless you, and in multiplying I will multiply your descendants like the stars of the heavens and like the sand on the seashore. And your seed (son/heir) will possess the gate of His enemies."

Abraham's profound faith introduced us to God as a provider! Abraham's faith bears much fruit and solidifies generational blessings that would be passed down through his descendants. His one action of surrender had a ripple effect, and we are still experiencing that today! We serve a God who provides. It's His name, His character, and His desire to provide.

So, what has this got to do with prosperity?

Why did I need to go into so much detail about this founding father of our faith?

Why am I asking you to consider covenant as the starting point to prosperity?

Well, as I said at the beginning, the covenant is about living out prosperity as our inheritance. It is also a hugely foundational piece of learning to take God at His word.

Covenantal Inheritance and Generational Wealth

Generational wealth is anything of value that is passed down. As believers, we must acknowledge that the first transfer of generational wealth started with Abraham, Isaac, and Jacob. Today, family remains the first framework God chose to establish circles of growing the kingdom of covenant promises, a cyclical economy of blessing from a cyclical God.

I believe that He gave us this example of how generational wealth is transferred so we could learn from it and follow it. This is not a biological rite of passage, but a spiritual inheritance. God does not require you to be biologically related to Abraham, Isaac, or Jacob to experience the financial promises, wealth, and blessings given to these patriarchs and descendants. It is an intimate joy to start really having this level of faith in our everyday lives.

Dig in Your Heels

Inherited Covenantal Blessing

Ask God to reveal to you what you have inherited.

We know that humans are broken and do broken things, but with the help of the Holy Spirit, may God reveal and restore to you what you have inherited down the line of biological parents, caretakers, and spiritual parents. Think of character traits, spiritual practices, and faith truths that have been received and expanded in your own life.

For example, I have mentioned that my mother was a Pentecostal praying woman as I was growing up. She taught me the power of prayer from an early age as well as the power of faith, despite so much abuse and hardship. I recognize prayer and faith as an inherited covenantal blessing from my mom.

Write a list of the following people in your journal and make a note of what covenantal blessings you have received from them either physically or spiritually.

Mother, father, grandmother, grandfather, spiritual father/mother. Add any significant family members that will add to this part of your testimony.

This is no joke. We have got to claim our inheritance in ways that we never might have seen before, and know that it is this with which we sow into the next generation.

Breakthrough Declarations and Decrees – Covenant

I'm a covenant believer.

I receive the blessing of Abraham on my life and family line in Jesus's name!

"Blessed are all who fear the Lord, who walk in obedience to Him. 2 You will eat the fruit of your labor; blessings and prosperity will be yours. 3 Your wife will be like a fruitful vine within your house; your children will be like olive shoots around your table." (Psalm 128 v 1-3)

I ask you, Lord, for healing in my soul (mind, will, and emotions) from any and all pain inflicted on me through the devastation of poverty. You have redeemed me from poverty and lack.

I break covenant with any and all verbal agreements to poverty and lack in the name of Jesus.

"But the meek will inherit the land and enjoy peace and prosperity." (Psalm 37 v 11)

CHAPTER 3 – The Power of Words

"Gentle words bring life and health; a deceitful tongue crushes the spirit."

Proverbs 15 v 4

"In the beginning was the Word, and the Word was with God."

John 1 v 1

I am a red-letter woman, and if there is one thing that I have come to know, it's that Jesus keeps things very simple. He spoke in parables to a people who lived and worked the land, and He often used the land as the teacher itself! Ok, I get it—as a people not living and working the land, we certainly have a tough time fully comprehending what was meant at times, but the principles are the same.

The words of Jesus don't hold back any punches, either. He asked more questions than gave answers and spoke words of the prophets in real time, not only showing his Judaic upbringing and the importance of the study of the Word but also declaring who He was by his actions. He fulfilled the "Law" (the Torah—literally "instructions" in biblical Hebrew), which meant he was an embodied completion of all the promises and instructions given by God. He was and is the living Word.

As a truth teller, Jesus's life looked like God's kingdom and sounded like God's kingdom, and after His seeds were sown and His purpose complete in death and resurrection, His life looked like covenantal expansion! Jesus lived a life of kingdom principles and set a precedent for a culture that looked like freedom, healing, love, friendship, and faith! Because we know so much about Abraham now and have explored his role as a father of the faith, we can have a greater understanding of who Jesus is and his life of prosperity. That's right, Jesus lived a life of prosperity, and if you feel challenged by that, go back to our definitions list and see if you agree.

Quick Truth

Jesus's life looked like God's kingdom and sounded like God's kingdom, and after His seeds were sown and His purpose complete in death and resurrection, His life looked like covenantal expansion!

The Cave and the Fields

Coming from where I come from, someone who was born in extreme poverty, I need you to know that I was never "supposed" to be where I am today. It was a revelation of radical faith and the Father's heart of God in my life, taking Him at His word, and decreeing His truth that led me to this place of living covenantal inheritance, wealth, and prosperity. Let me give you a little more background.

I was born in a cave in a village in Mexico where there was a culture of rivalry, distrust, abuse, and poverty. My mother worked the fields amongst the livestock just to put food on the table and her story was one of hardship. You see, there were rival families in the village where my mom grew up in, and she ended up being kidnapped by the son of the rival family. She was given five children by this man, but her own family thought she had run off with him. This, however, was no Romeo and Juliet. This was dysfunction and abuse on another level. When she finally returned to her family, she would be treated like "the help" to earn her keep. For her, the cycle of poverty and abuse felt impossible to break through, and this was the environment I was born into.

The first months of my life were ones of neglect, as I was left at home while my mother went to work. It wasn't until one of my sisters visited that I was taken to a city at nine months old, my birth was registered, and my life had the potential for change. You can never underestimate the small choices that are made around you on your behalf, and this compassionate action meant the future could potentially look different. Of course, this wasn't the end of the story. My mother worked five jobs, my father was a raging alcoholic, and yet, amongst the chaos, my mother taught us that our poverty did not have to be our destiny. My mother was the first example I had of what it means to be a generous and Godly sower of seeds.

My mother taught us that even though we were poor, we didn't need to be dirty; even though we were poor, we could still have dignity; even though we were poor, our word was our bond. And there it was! "The word was our bond." It's only now when I recount these words that I realize she was teaching us the profound truths of God's ways, for God's word is His bond. His word was the way He created, expanded, and made promises to His people that He would never leave them or forsake them. It was His word! So, there I was, living in prosperity and wealth without a dime to my name but with a revelation of what we really had access to in God's economy. At a young age, I was learning to live a faith that believed every word of the covenantal promises and my spiritual inheritance.

There is a book called The Circle Maker. It talks in depth about the prayer circles that we can make around our dreams as well as our fears. I had been praying in this way long before this book was released, and I was so encouraged by how it was explained by Mark Batterson, the author. I really think that this method of decree and declaration gave me a faith-strong foundation to my walk with God and was a huge part of my upbringing and the way that my mom prayed too. I am grateful for her every day for her example in my life.

Faith, Poverty, and Unbelief

The scriptures give us a lot of examples and wisdom when it comes to how words can bring life or death, and I want to take a quick moment to stress the point. As I learned from a young age, words have power and when Jesus taught His disciples about faith, He emphasized the importance of the words we speak and pray. He also led with some pretty powerful examples like the time He cursed a fig tree and then followed up with this mic drop of truth about the economy of words in God's kingdom. It seems these days that we been conditioned to be mountain climbers when God called us to be mountain movers.

"Truly I tell you, if anyone says to this mountain, 'Go, throw yourself into the sea,' and does not doubt in their heart but believes that what they say will happen, it will be done for them. Therefore I tell you, whatever you ask for in prayer, believe that you have received it, and it will be yours." Mark 11 v 23–24

Many times our blessings, such as healing or prosperity, are blocked because we are speaking words of unbelief. We should not be counteracting our own faith with faithless speech; it only breeds unbelief. Look, the fundamental key to the seed is that it spends a lot of time in the dark, dying to itself, and a lot of us miss not only our breakthrough but our harvest, too, because we get impatient with the waiting. We get discouraged during the germination process of our seed because it looks like nothing is happening, but in reality, most of the transformation of our seed is done in the darkest of soil/times in our lives. This is a crucial part of the transformation process of the seed. When we speak words that are self-sabotage, they can cause us to delay or lose the blessings ordained to be received in a specific, set-apart time. Many times God wants to grant us the desires of our heart, but our unbelief blocks this, and our lack of patience in the waiting kills the potential.

I want to suggest that unbelief is a result of poverty, and poverty is a bondage if you embrace a slavery mentality by confirming it with your lips. The only outcome will be that you will feel well and truly cornered by your circumstances. Later in this book, I will tell you more about the revelation God gave my heart and mind about the kingdom of heaven being a method of overflow. You may end up being surprised by what landed in my spirit, but for now let's stick with the subject of seeds and words.

If we pray for God's blessings and know from the Word that He wants to bless us, then what we say should reflect that. All this looked like something in my life. I knew the principles and power of declaring the covenantal promises over my own life and others. I would fast and pray and see miracles happen. I will never forget as a twelve-year-old girl praying for a friend whose green card was denied. I fasted and declared a way where there seemed to be no way. Two weeks later, he received a letter saying that there had been a mistake and he had been granted a green card. God is just so super cool!

Dig in Your Heels – Words

Where could you have influence? How do you use your words to uplift others? Why not have some fun and write a few notes of encouragement to friends or family members? Use your words to edify others and sow into their lives, praying that they will be inspired to live fruitfully in the coming season.

Breakthrough Declarations and Decrees

I come against the words that have sought to destroy and discourage me in my walk with God.

I renounce all the ways that I have used my words to destroy and discourage others.

I declare wisdom to be on my lips when communicating with others.

I speak out words of life over my own life and all those around me.

"Evil words destroy one's friends; wise discernment rescues the godly." Proverbs 11 v 9

"Your own soul is nourished when you are kind, but you destroy yourself when you are cruel." Proverbs 11 v 17

"Gentle words bring life and health; a deceitful tongue crushes the spirit." Proverbs 15 v 4

"A person's words can be life-giving water; words of true wisdom are as refreshing as a bubbling brook." Proverbs 18 v 4

CHAPTER 4 – The Power of Mindset

"Therefore, with minds that are alert and fully sober, set your hope on the grace to be brought to you when Jesus Christ is revealed at his coming."

1 Peter 1 v 13

"Do not conform to the pattern of this world, but be transformed by the renewing of your mind. Then you will be able to test and approve what God's will is - his good, pleasing, and perfect will."

Romans 12 v 2

It was a setup. The weight and confusion of feeling rejected fell heavy on my heart, but as with everything God has journeyed me through, I knew I was being primed for an experience of healing and breakthrough. The only difficulty? That I would have to walk through it! The greatest challenge: remembering the power I held around mindset.

The experiences in my childhood of having an abusive, drunk father impacted me greatly when it came to rejection. There was an assignment of rejection over my life from the moment I was born and I had to live every day in the knowledge that I had a father who didn't want me. The thing is, though, as much as this was my everyday reality, and I was very aware of it, I knew it was not going to be a place that I would stay.

As a child, there was something that I knew deeply before my physical situation changed. I wonder if that's why God tells us to come to Him with a childlike faith, because as a child there seemed to be an innocence in my faith that as an adult I would probably now call boldness. As I walked with God, I learned not to take my father's brokenness personally; I didn't let the lies that he lived by get in my head, despite struggling with the familiar devil of rejection. Situations would come into my life that would torment me and the enemy would use these moments to try and reinforce my greatest fears around not being wanted, loved, accepted, and seen. Sometimes the battle would be short and sometimes it would take some time, but at the core of me, like an iron rod, I knew that my God was bigger than all of this. I believed that my heavenly Father conquered not only the physical realities of my childhood but also the thoughts that reinforced the spirit of rejection.

The reason why I am telling you all this is because this stuff is grit-and-guts hard at times. I have had to work on my mindsets around trust and bring this area of my life before God when it plagues me. Listen up, my friend: Rejection is the antithesis of prosperity, and breaking the mindset of poverty is the key to it all! I am not under any illusion that the process won't take time or lead us into some valleys, but think about it—a rejection spirit will hinder the blessing from being fully received, and a poverty mindset will be quite happy with that. For me, the process has looked like renewing my mind with the scriptures every morning. It has looked like a simple belief and a radical faith in the revelation of who the Father is and what I have access to in Him. It's all fundamentally connected to being transformed by the renewing of the mind and believing the blessing and inheritance of prosperity!

Quick Truth

Rejection is the antithesis of prosperity.

The Heart

It is worth noting that whenever you see the word "heart" in the scripture it can be equally translated as the word "mind," highlighting that translators didn't quite know what to do with the concept of this being a whole-being experience. Poverty is an attitude of the heart and the consequence of an unrenewed mind, all of which comes from within.

It is a development of our heart/mind that comes from the responses we make to the difficulties in our lives. Two people can go through the same experiences and suffer the same conditions of life and yet come out as entirely different people. One can succumb to these problems and become bitter, resentful, and moody. The other can come through these experiences and be a successful, happy, and generous person. It is not what happens to you that matters but what you do with what happens to you.

Poverty Heart/Mindset and Breaking the Chains

Our mind is a powerful part of who we are, and thought patterns can sometimes paralyze us with fear. An old memory can project on new experiences, trying to steer our attention away from what God says about us and to us through His word. Mindset plays a huge role in identity and learning to communicate well with both God and each other. It can also deeply affect how we sow seeds, practice generosity, and seek to live a life of prosperity.

The definition of the word "poverty" speaks about the lack of wealth that leads the human heart to beg. This is why the revelation of the Father's heart about the covenant promises, to me, makes so much sense, and I want to take this moment to say loud and clear: **"We don't need to beg for what we have already been given."**

This is the biggest lie of the poverty mindset and the root of the enemy's first and only tactic. In Genesis 3 v 1, the enemy starts with a question, and it's been the only one he has been asking since: "Did God really say, 'You must not eat from any tree in the garden'?" The Father's covenantal promises can't be revoked, even if man suffers with a bad case of the poverty mindset!

God made it so clear to me that a poverty mindset strongly influences the motivations and freedom of the heart. Poverty mindset leads to a lack of compassion and understanding and has the power to close the heart to His covenantal abundance. I feel in my spirit that the poverty-stricken heart suffers from a great lack of faith that stops a flow of generosity, forgiveness, and expansion, leading to devastating consequences. This is why an understanding of God's relationship with Abraham and Sarah is such a key revelation and why I started this book talking about their lives.

Abraham was the epitome of someone walking by faith, and God chose him to forge a new path of covenantal expansion. Up to that point poverty had looked like idols in his biological father's house, but here God was teaching Abraham about the Father heart of God and what it means to walk in His ways. A kingdom characterized by covenantal promises, compassion, and generative seed sowing.

Ultimately, a poverty mindset is most obvious when we try to live our lives enslaved to fear and close our hearts to the call of God. Other warning signs that a poverty mindset is ruling the roost can look and sound like being highly critical of others, having an ungrateful spirit, an unhealthy balance with regards to self-preservation, and a deep-seated selfishness. In a poverty mindset, we stop seeing and hearing as God does in our everyday lives and miss the cries of the people. It really is a sorry state of affairs.

So, how do we break the chains of a poverty mindset? Well, let's make a list and check it twice!

1. It is very important that we acknowledge where the power of poverty is manifesting in our lives.

Once you see it, you can't unsee it. Once it is named, it loses some of its power!

2. We need to ask for forgiveness and repent for the poverty mindset in our lives.

3. Through prayer, decree, and declaration we learn to ask Jesus, our salvation, to break off the chains of poverty.

4. We must guard our hearts from poverty mindsets creeping back into our lives. We can do this by having a spirit of giving, obedience, generosity, appreciation, compassion, and understanding. As a result, I believe that our attitudes and actions will look like having a generous spirit that aligns with God's purposes in the world.

As we change our minds around the subject of prosperity and wealth by the power of the Spirit, poverty mindsets wither away. They lose their power and leave us feeling free. Many resources highlight that it takes between forty and fifty days to create a new mindset, so have patience and be persistent with the changing of your thoughts and actions in this area.

Dig in Your Heels – Mindset

Breaking poverty mindsets starts with the heart/mind and learning to tell a different story.

Take a moment to think of a personal experience that has happened in your life or is happening in your life.

What is true about this experience and what is false? Learning to accurately observe our lives with the support and power of the Holy Spirit is part of building a mindful set of memories based on truth and integrity.

What stories have you told that have not been seeds of truth? What do you need to turn from (repent for) and make efforts to change as you tell your story?

God says all the way through scripture to remember, remember, remember. Remember your story to the covenant and the inheritance that is available to you.

Breakthrough Declarations and Decrees

I renounce every mentality and mindset I've inherited that's rooted in mediocrity and poverty.

I loose myself from all ignorance and knowledge blocking strongholds concerning prosperity and financial increase in Jesus's name.

I renounce every mindset that has come to destroy the work of God in my life.

I declare I am and will be transformed by the renewing of my mind by the power of the Holy Spirit in Jesus's name.

CHAPTER 5 – The Power of Awakening

"For anything that becomes visible is light. Therefore it says, 'Awake, O sleeper, and arise from the dead, and Christ will shine on you.' "

Ephesians 5 v 14

"Humble yourselves before the Lord, and he will lift you up."

James 4 v 10

A Rude Awakening

Or as I like to call it, a Ruth Awakening!

As I have mentioned, I have been just as much a student around the subject of covenantal prosperity and wealth as the next person, and the following story is of one of those moments God brought me to my own Mt. Moriah (God is teacher) that was a catalyst for change around the subject of money.

One night, my four-year-old son (who is now an adult) and I came home, opened our front door, and flipped on the light switch; the house remained dark. I tried another switch, and it didn't work either. Then it hit me like a ton of bricks: The power company had made good on their threats to shut off my electricity due to nonpayment.

Thinking quickly, I told my son, "Let's play a game. Let's see if we can get ready for bed in the dark, only using a flashlight." My son Darian giggled, put his Spiderman and Hot Wheels in his pockets, and happily agreed to the challenge. Looking back now it was a fun moment of adventure, but deep down I was asking for God to turn on a light for me to see more clearly what was going on. The next day, I renegotiated a payment plan with the company and got my power restored. We really were living hand to mouth and the lessons kept on rolling in.

A few months later, I woke up one morning and was about to leave for work but my car was not in the parking space. I ran back into the house and called the police to frantically report my car was stolen! It was such an awful moment of panic. After putting me on a brief hold, the police dispatcher returned and said, "Ma'am, your car was repossessed." What makes this story so incredulous is that my husband and I had jobs, but he was working for a startup company raising capital and some months he wouldn't get paid at all. I knew how to be frugal with finances, but I hated living that way. I became a master in making every dime count and honestly felt pretty proud of myself for my extreme thriftiness.

With a mindset around money fully locked and loaded, we did a lot of surviving. With a young family and investing time and energy in new ventures, we just trusted that we would make ends meet at the close of each month. Honestly, our faith was strong, but our willpower to make things work seemed stronger, and that's why the revelation about covenant and kingdom prosperity was such a lifesaver.

Our story of financial wealth has not been a straight line. It has been up-and-down; we have been walking through fire one moment and the next seeing mountains move. We walked by faith, holding up our hands to a God who kept on providing. We were grateful; I was grateful for the gracious ways God kept on showing up. However, after living this way for a few years, I realized that my mindset around money was sabotaging any chances I had of achieving real wealth and setting a solid financial example for my kids.

So, I told God that I need to be reminded of His promises and that I was going to exercise kingdom principles. These principles changed my life and have been the driving force of all my financial decisions since. I surrendered each part of our finances to God and learned how to pray for not only what we needed but what we wanted. I would sow with intention and would expect a harvest in our lives. The fun thing is that God taught us and showed up again and again as we learned to have a kingdom-oriented money mindset.

Remember what I said at the beginning of this book? If I ask God for what I want, I will never have a need again. This truly became our reality, and I have been in awe of how God uses the things we ask for in the building and for the glory of His kingdom.

What Did This Look like in Real Time?

As I have hinted at, this didn't happen overnight, but it did start to happen in small ways and over time it all started to add up. I feel like we were better resourced to make practical changes now that a revelation of God's covenant plan was leading the show. I started tithing, stopped using credit cards for consumer purchases, sent my son to private schools and college without requiring him to get loans, bought my house in cash, obtained a perfect credit score, and became an even bigger giver.

Quick Truth

Unless I manage my money according to God's word—the one who owns it all—I'll never have true wealth or peace in my finances.

I am proud to say that I became an expert in godly financial principles because I lived it out loud and on purpose! I also realized that no matter what worldly knowledge I obtained about money and wealth, unless I managed my money according to God's word—the one who owns it all—I'd never have true wealth or peace in my finances.

Changing the way you think about money is the single greatest thing you can do to make a difference in your current situation. The good news is once you replace your false mindset with the truth, you can position yourself to obtain and maintain wealth and enjoy the life of prosperity you were designed for.

Debunking the Myth

Many people can get stuck in the thinking that if they just made more money or hit the Powerball, then all their financial problems would go away, but research shows that those who get rich quickly, or even those who retire from big-money professional sports, can end up declaring bankruptcy within just a few years. Having more money can lead to all kinds of problems because finances without faith is a recipe for disaster. It's why I am so passionate about sharing my story and putting such a huge emphasis on mindset.

Returning

Awakening to the ways of God's kingdom has kept me teachable, humble, and open to the changes that have needed to happen to realign to His covenant promises. In my sin, God has met me and tenderly loved me back into position before His throne. The greatest love I have felt from Him has been when I have not been perfect. I mean, who is, right?! I guess the point I want to make, though, is that every day can be different, and His grace abounds when I am not living up to the potential of who I am and what He has placed in me to bring to the world. Knowing the depths of His love, acceptance, and nurturing is a game changer. At my worst, He is His best. At my weakest, He is my strength.

Dig in Your Heels — Awakening

Many beliefs are so buried in our subconscious that we aren't aware of them. Until you wake up to these limiting beliefs, it will be hard to change your mindset. Set aside some quiet time to really focus on this exercise. It can help you uncover your false mindset about prosperity in the area of money and change it. I need you to be radically honest and courageous.

Think about some of your earliest attitudes, thoughts, and beliefs about money. Focus on things you were told, or things you observed your parents say or do when it came to money. Also consider any emotionally charged or dramatic events associated with money that have left a lasting mark on you. Write down as many as you can.

As you continue reading the book, come back to your list when you read a biblical principle or scripture that counters an old thought pattern. Scratch out the old belief and write in a new one.

Read "The Parable of the Talents" in Matthew 25 v 14-30 and ask the Holy Spirit to reveal truths.

Breakthrough Declarations and Decrees

I come against the powers of darkness that have imposed poverty in my life and I break the shackles of poverty in Jesus's name.

I renounce all greed, covetousness, and lust for things associated with poverty.

I renounce every power of poverty that seeks to keep the windows of heaven closed over my life. I close every door, every gate, opening, and access point to the spirit of poverty and lack against my life in Jesus's name!

I declare freedom over my life in Jesus's name when it comes to the slavery of an unGodly wealth mindset.

CHAPTER 6 – The Power of Source
Covenant or Credit Cards

"The rich rule over the poor, and the borrower is a slave to the lender."

Proverbs 22 v 7

Before I go too much further, I want to bring up a very practical conversation about credit cards. I observe that many are suffering in the church because of credit cards and the debt they create in people's lives. I also feel like the subject of credit must be addressed, especially in the context of seeds, sowing, and the growth of kingdom prosperity. Let's dive in!

Like we did with the conversation around inheritance, I want you to take a couple of minutes to think about how your family handled finances. Journal some of the ways that finances were managed in your home. Were you exposed to conversations about finances? Was there tension in your home around money? Did you parents or caregivers teach you about how to handle money from a young age? Were you aware of credit cards being used in your family economy?

There is no condemnation here; it's just important to get some personal context around this subject so you can act accordingly and learn how to teach your kids not to live beyond their means and rely on credit with a quick-fix mentality.

Let's start slow. Have you ever thought about why money is called a "currency"? Well, it's very simple, really—it has to flow! Financial resources are designed to flow in and out of our lives with ease and purpose. In the context of covenantal blessing, we know that the source of all blessings comes truly and only from God. The thing with credit cards is that the source changes! We sign our names to a source of a false wealth which, in fact, is just an illusion. Again, this is why remembering our covenantal position is so key and why I believe the enemy has a field day using credit cards to keep us in bondage.

When it comes to our monetary resources, I need you to hear this right in the gut: Credit cards are not prosperity and they should not be the source of our seeds. I know it might feel hard to read that, but it's true. I have been shocked by what I have heard from the pulpit around this very subject.

A number of years ago I was part of a church that was raising money for a new building. I can still hear the preacher's voice in my head: "Put it on the card, trust God to pay for it later." On the one hand I couldn't believe what I was hearing, but on the other I was like, "Here is an agenda, and this guy needs to succeed!" I got it; it just felt a bit gross that he treated the flock in this way and had the power to potentially influence the whole culture of this faith community. I couldn't help but think what a genetically modified church we were becoming while preaching a genetically minimized gospel! It might seem like I am being hard-edged on this, but I feel like a gospel preached in this way only minimizes God's promises of abundance and blessing. The genetically minimized gospel inserts man's agenda and interprets scripture away from the context of God's covenantal story. This stuff has to be taken seriously.

The confusing thing in the midst of all this is that the subject of "faith" was actually being preached, just in a distorted way. When you ask people to use credit cards, you are engaging in a culture that is not rooted in the covenant blessings of God. It really is that simple. Even now as I write about this experience, it feels like faith bounced around the auditorium that morning like a pinball machine, leaving some people confused on what to do. I really do know that it can feel easier to buy now and pay later, but this is the epitome of a false economy, and the "balance" literally and figuratively needs addressing.

Getting Painfully Practical with Credit Cards

Let's start with the credit card basics. We all know that when you use credit rather than cash to make consumer purchases (clothing, food, home items, entertainment, electronics, etc.), it allows you to live beyond your means, buy beyond your means, and increases the chance of impulse buying. The bottom line: It is not easier to buy now and pay later, because financial charges mean you will be paying and paying again later!

Finance charges are fees or interest the credit card company charges for the convenience of delaying payment. They are basically lending you the money, which you pay back and incrementally. The longer you take to pay it back, the greater the interest fees you pay. Don't fool yourself and say, "I'll put it on my charge card and pay it in full before interest charges hit." If you're willing to do that, you would have paid in full at the point of purchase. It's too easy and tempting to just pay the minimum due each month, which causes you to end up paying for the item twice or three times over.

Quick Truth

Credit cards are not prosperity and they should not be the source of our seeds.

What's the Real Cost of a Credit Card?

This might be obvious to you, but I think it's worth going through some figures in real time. You know, just to get our head in some of this credit card reality. Here's an example that you can apply to just about anything you are buying on credit.

You decide you want a new sofa. Rather than waiting to save up the money for it, you decide to put it on a credit card that already has a $1,500 balance on it from previous purchases. The sofa is $3,000, so your new balance on the credit card is $4,500. The monthly finance charge can be calculated by knowing four things:

Credit card balance = $4,500

Annual percentage rate (APR) = 24%

Length of billing cycle = 12 months

Periodic rate equals APR divided by billing cycles equals .24 / 12 = 0.02

Your monthly finance charge is $4,500 x .02 = $90

Are you still with me?

This $90 is in addition to the cost of the items you purchased with the credit card. So, if you pay $150, only $60 goes toward knocking down your balance. The other $90 is the cost of borrowing that you pay the credit card company. So even though you paid your $150, your new balance is $4,440—just $60 less than what it was, because you had to pay the credit card company $90. Next month, you'll have another finance charge to pay based on your balance of $4,440. As long as you have a balance on your credit card, you will have to pay finance charges each month and will end up giving the credit card company much more than the original cost of the sofa. It would have been better to not buy the new sofa or to wait until you had enough cash to save to buy it outright.

When it comes to consumer type purchases, I strongly advise that you never use credit. Train yourself to be present to what you have, and practice delayed gratification and only purchasing when you have enough cash to do so. Interestingly, research has shown that delayed gratification is one of the most effective personality traits of prosperous people. In summary, when purchasing consumer goods, buying now and paying later is one of the most cunning of all money traps! For larger purchases like a car or home, financing is likely necessary and expected, but you should still use wisdom to minimize the cost of borrowing.

Honestly, we could talk a lot about the world's way of doing finance, but right now I want to draw your mind back to the word of God and what scripture offers us. After all, if our minds continue to be transformed from right action and obedience to God's word, we will see a natural flow of kingdom principles in every area of our lives.

What Wisdom Does the Bible Give Us on Debt and Borrowing?

As you have already heard about one of my own personal (rude) awakenings, I have not always got this "right," but one thing I know is God does not want His children to be ruled over or to be slaves of any other kingdom but His. However, the scriptures tell us the story of slavery to freedom is a very real cycle in the human experience.

Do you ever have those moments when you are reading scripture and a revelation by the Holy Spirit feels like a punch in your gut? Well, a few years ago I came across this scripture in Romans 13 v 8 and it literally exploded in my spirit and helped transform my mind, my thinking around debt and credit cards. The word of God clearly said to me:

"Owe nothing to anyone except to love one another; for the one who loves his neighbor has fulfilled the Law."

Romans 13 v 8

"Owe nothing to anyone, except to love . . ." This simple phrase forced me to look at debt in a completely different way. The fullness of the verse also led me back to our covenantal relationship with God and what that means when it comes to a debt-free inheritance. You see, debt makes us slaves. We are slaves to the person (or bank) we owe, and all we are commanded to acquire is love. That's why Paul says in Romans 1 v 14, "I am debtor both to the Greeks and to the barbarians; both to the wise and to the unwise." He was speaking about the debt he felt in sharing with them the gospel of Christ because God had so blessed him above measure. Paul felt himself a debtor to the lost world. That is love! It is a gospel debt: a debt of good news, a debt that can only be paid by getting the gospel to others any way we can. Owing another person or system something other than covenantal love is dangerous ground for gospel dwellers to live because it limits us in so many ways.

Just to touch on the end of Paul's words in Romans, the word "law" in biblical Hebrew is the literal word "instruction, teaching, and to hit the mark." It is a word that reminds us to be a people of obedience, right action, and prophetic declaration. What I love about this verse in Romans is that it teaches us another level of what it means to love in a covenantal way. After all, love is a covenantal word that should be at the heart of prosperity and God's kingdom expansion. You may be asking, "Why can we have confidence in this?" Well, the word "love" doesn't appear in scripture until the story of Abraham and Isaac. This kind of love is father-son. This kind of love is about the future.

Another couple of scriptures that I felt reiterated these truths are in Deuteronomy 15 and 28.

"For the Lord your God will bless you as he has promised, and you will lend to many nations but will borrow from none. You will rule over many nations but none will rule over you."

Deuteronomy 15 v 6

"The Lord will open the heavens, the storehouse of his bounty, to send rain on your land in season and to bless all the work of your hands. You will lend to many nations but will borrow from none."

Deuteronomy 28 v 12

Goodness, can we let these truths sink in and be the motivation to ready ourselves for a prosperous life? You're a child of the highest King, and you have access to all that He has dominion over, all that is His. But these blessings will be hindered when you're mired in the vicious cycle of debt. Practice obedience and discipline in the area that says "NO!" to debt. Meditate on this truth and commit to eliminating credit cards as a common form of payment for goods and services. Your goal is to be the lender, not the borrower, and the giver from the blessings that God has poured out on your life.

What Does the Bible Say about Wealth?

Finally, it has been said that there are over two thousand verses about wealth/finances in the Bible. There are more scriptures about finances and prosperity than about salvation, healing, grace, and mercy; that tells me that God wants to let us know that prosperity is within God's design for our lives. My understanding is that this includes references to gold, silver, and wealth in belongings, communal wealth (think the building of the tabernacle and the disciples' life on the road), and the challenges that face all humanity when it comes to loving money over loving God.

I hope that this chapter has been helpful when it comes to addressing the curse of debt and that you are encouraged to repent and return to the kingdom covenant principles of God. I hope in the seasons ahead you will feel empowered when it comes to managing your finances in a Godly way.

Dig in Your Heels – Credit Cards

Go grab your credit card statements and just take a moment to look at the charges you are paying. Take some time to pray and use the breakthrough declarations and decrees to break off any false ideas you have.

Circle your debt and declare grace and favor over the amount, and take some time to pray and set goals to pay off your debt.

Breakthrough Declarations and Decrees

Lord break the brass heavens above me and the iron earth beneath. I renounce all dependency on bank cards, credit cards, store cards, and the like. I decree grace for kingdom stewardship and grace concerning finances comes upon me in Jesus's name!

I renounce every financial sanction and financial restraint over my life that would seek to confine me in Jesus's name.

Lord, you are my source. I renounce every spendthrift spirit that seeks to hold me captive through lack of discipline in Jesus's name! I repent for using credit cards to gain beyond the means you have given me. Teach me to trust you and be comfortable with waiting for new desired items.

I renounce allegiances to every financial taskmaster I covenanted with through contracts, compounded interest, high-risk loans, and revolving debt. I speak freedom over my life. I come out of agreement with every work of destruction linked to poverty. I sever the connections and proclaim freedom over my life. Freedom from debt, scarcity, and financial failure in Jesus's name!

CHAPTER 7 – The Power of Kingdom Method

"I tell you the truth, if you have faith as small as mustard seed you can say to this mountain, 'Move from here to there,' and it will move. Nothing will be impossible for you."

Matthew 17 v 20 (NIV)

"Children, how hard it is to enter the kingdom of God! It is easier for a camel to go through the eye of a needle than for someone who is rich to enter the kingdom of God."

Mark 10 v 24-25

"But my God shall supply all your needs according to His riches in glory by Christ Jesus."

Philippians 4 v 19

Quite literally the biggest revelation—after that of coming face-to-face with the reality of covenantal inheritance—has been that the kingdom of heaven is NOT a destination but a METHOD! I don't believe simply that God's kingdom is about a final destination in heaven. It's not! "On earth as it is in heaven" is the line from the Lord's Prayer that is a statement and communication to action in the here and now. It is a way to pray that tells me that the kingdom of heaven is the heartbeat method of God's ways on earth NOW! We have got to stop believing that we are just "passing through" this world with an exclusive destination.

As you know from my early exploration of the word "prosperity," I love language and the nuances hidden in the definition of words. The definition of "method" is really juicy when you explore its meaning, so I collated a few descriptions here for you to see. I really value doing exercises like this, as it always broadens my view of how God uses words to expand His kingdom.

Method: *a set of methods, rules, or ideas that are important in a science or art, a particular procedure, or set of procedures.*

Synonyms for method*: approach, fashion, form, how, manner, methodology, recipe, strategy, style, system, tack, tactics, technique, way.*

Words related to method: *mode, modus operandi, blueprint, design, game plan, game, ground plan, intrigue, layout, line, model, plan, program, route, scheme, expedient, move, shift, step, practice, process, routine, policy.*

Do you see how fun it is to really dive into a word? What an amazing descriptive bunch of words connected to method. Just by looking at them and thinking about how we even use them in our everyday lives is so expansive. That's how I know that the kingdom of heaven is not a final destination but a method. God's way of doing things are the manner by which we live and breathe the blueprint here on earth! Have a play around with the words and see how the Spirit inspires you to see the kingdom of God being a method that is tangible and real. Write them down and even stick them on your fridge door or somewhere you go each day to remind you of the kingdom method here on earth.

Engaging the Method

The kingdom of God is a completely different set of cultural norms than that of the way we do things on earth in the power and motives of man. Heaven moves and you engage in faith when you pray for what you cannot see but still want—it's a completely different approach. Kingdom as method is a transformed mindset. It starts with a declaration of all the ways needs are met; it's a declaration of gratitude that spills out into every area of our lives. Look, as I was saying to a friend the other day, I don't waste precious spiritual energy on praying for my needs to be met. God has already told us that He will meet all the needs of His people. With that piece in place, I then simply and boldly engage in the principle of asking God for what I want because of His love for me and my attitude of prosperity to see His kingdom shine. And let me tell you, if I can do it, you can too. By engaging with the simple principle of radical faith and giving, sowing, and reaping, I am where I am. There is no magic trick; it is just about purposefully investing time, money, and energy in the things that matter to you and choosing the joy of gratefulness in the small and the big things, however they fall on your field.

The kingdom of God is a method, to me, in many different ways. I describe part of the method as targeted prayer that encircles the thing I am praying for, whether that be a circumstance or something physical. It then looks like pulling down the reality of its wholeness (prosperity) from the spiritual realm with a level of faith that can sometimes look darn right crazy. In fact, my husband, Eric, calls it "stupid faith," which does make me smile, because sometimes what I am praying for is pretty wild. Folks, this is about the fundamental principle of kingdom living and the real-life experience of it here on earth. It's gonna look like crazy stupid faith in the eyes of those who have not grasped the instruction to take God at His word. For some reason, this truth does take a lot for people to really hear and, in hearing, to really LIVE!

I want to put it another way, because honestly, this is how I see Jesus lived His life. He walked around as the embodied nature of God's kingdom on earth and as the living breathing testimony of covenant promise. I have a preacher's voice in my head saying, "Can I get a witness?" because I feel like this is what Jesus was really asking everywhere He went. "Can I get a witness? Because I am living what God has always said was possible, and I wonder if you can see it!" His ministry was short in so many ways, and I believe that people must have loved being around him while he was growing up. He was a student longer than he was a teacher or leader of his hand-picked disciples, and he worked as a carpenter longer than he was healing blind beggars, bleeding women, and demonically possessed kids. Jesus simply lived in accordance with what he had faith for and taught from a place of storytelling and loving kindness that really was about pulling the kingdom of heaven to earth.

Quick Truth

I don't waste spiritual energy on praying for my needs to be met. God has already told us that He will meet all the needs of His people.

The Parable of the Rich Young Ruler

Following on from this revelation of the kingdom of God being a method and not a destination, I wanted to share some thoughts that came to light as I was reading the encounter that Jesus had with a rich young ruler in Mark 10 v 17-27. This intriguing story talks about wealth with a warning, and I think that it holds some pearls of wisdom and a helpful angle on the kingdom method. If you have your Bible close, take a few moments to read the story in Mark's Gospel. While you are reading it, journal any questions that you might have and ask the Holy Spirit to unveil its wisdom and soften your heart to receive its truths.

I have noticed how many believers read this scripture in Mark and end up thinking to themselves, "I better not become rich if I plan on going to heaven because of how Jesus talked to the rich man." However, what we have to bear in mind is that Jesus was being typically Rabbinic in style and countercultural in content. For Jesus to say it was hard for a rich man to enter God's kingdom was countercultural because people had an entitled belief system that wealth equaled the approval and blessing of God. This then led to people believing they were more special because they were rich, and they thought that was enough. Jesus wanted to readjust people's mindsets back to righteousness and kingdom covenantal prosperity, and here again he used the physical proximity and land to teach.

Quick Truth

Jesus was being typically Rabbinic in style and countercultural in content.

As it turns out, there was—and still is (although not used for trade)—a very narrow gate in Jerusalem that was used by people in ancient days to enter the city. This gate was nicknamed the Eye of the Needle and was quite tricky for large, heavily ladened camels to pass through since it was so small. In ancient days, the main form of transport in the Middle East would have been camels, and all who travelled and traded would have owned one (or many). There are a number of commentaries and interpretations of this encounter with the rich man. The camel through the Eye of the Needle is just such a great picture! Could Jesus simply have meant that, far from being impossible, it was merely tricky to enter the kingdom of heaven? The gate is so small that baggage on the camel's back had to be removed, and then as well as that, the camel needed to stoop down in order to fit through it. I think Jesus is using imagery to let the Hebrews know that being rich doesn't guarantee entrance to heaven, and like the camel wouldn't fit through the gate ladened with possessions, there is a sense that a rich man would have to unload his possessions to go through the narrow gate. Think about it—he wasn't called a prosperous man, he was called a rich man. They are different.

The scripture in Mark conveys to us that if you desire to enter God's kingdom, then you must be willing to lay down your possessions and be ready to enter in a kingdom way. To get low, and to have a humble heart, and you know when you humble yourself unto God's almighty's hand, He will lift you up in His perfect timing. To me this passage teaches that it's easier for a rich man to enter the Eye of the Needle (man's way of doing things) than to enter the kingdom of heaven (God's way of doing things), and we must make a decision as to what kingdom we will serve. I love this verse in 1 Peter 5 v 6. May it be an encouragement to you in this process.

"Humble yourselves, therefore, under God's mighty hand, that he may lift you up in due time. Cast all your anxiety on him because he cares for you."

1 Peter 5 v 6

How Do We Pray/Ask for What God Has Already Promised Us?

This is a great question to ask as we learn the ways of kingdom prosperity in our lives. In 1 Kings 3 v 5, the Lord appears to King Solomon in a dream and says to him, "Ask what I shall give you." To me, this is the most radically wise and simple form of prayer when it comes to asking God for what He has already promised us, and we all know that King Solomon goes on to be rather wealthy in many areas of his life. Of course, his story comes with a bunch of lessons and invites us into a conversation about biblical wisdom in general, the dos, and the don'ts, but this interaction sets a precedent for supernatural prosperity and growth.

The Power of Attorney

One final aspect to this kingdom method that I want to share is what it means to give someone the power of attorney. This document is an agreement between two parties that means one can act fully on behalf of the other. If you give me power of attorney, for example, I become you from a legal point of view. I can sell your house and you don't even have to be there. I can tap into your bank accounts, even, because as far as the government is concerned, I am with you and I have access to all your assets and not necessarily your liabilities.

The point I want to make about this part of the kingdom method is the power of attorney we received when we got saved, the power of the name of Jesus. Interestingly, it didn't start there either. In Exodus 23 v 21, God says to the people of Israel He will send an angel before the people to protect them along the way and bring them to a place that He has prepared. It comes with just one caveat: that the people walk in His ways, in His kingdom principles, as an example to the nations as a people set apart—a people that are us!

Dig in Your Heels – Kingdom Method

Go back to the questions and notes that you took when you read the passage about the rich young ruler in Mark.

What do you see as the differences between being rich and being prosperous?

Do you relate to the rich young ruler?

How might asking God for what you want while removing what is not needed play out in your everyday life?

Breakthrough Declarations and Decrees

Read Psalm 27 as a declaration and decree.

CHAPTER 8 – The Power of Seeds

"As long as the earth endures, seedtime and harvest, cold and heat, summer and winter, day and night, will never cease."

Genesis 8 v 22 (NIV)

"Do not be deceived, God is not mocked; for whatever a man sows, that he will also reap."

Matthew 17 v 20 (NIV)

"But the seed falling on good soil refers to someone who hears the word and understands it. This is the one who produces a crop, yielding a hundred, sixty, or thirty times what was sown."

Matthew 13 v 23 (NIV)

The seeds of our lives are anything that you give for purpose on purpose and sometimes even unconsciously by just being who you are. Seeds could be time, money, hope, resources, faith, love—the list is endless, really. They could also be seeds of encouragement, the seeds that are a sign that tells the person, organization, business, that you believe in them and that you see them. The seed of trust and the seed of joy; all these seeds that have the potential to bring forth life and a harvest that will feed those around you, including the next generation. The seeds of our lives are prayers of our lives. They are a beautiful way of communicating with God and with each other. They make us closer.

I have seen so many people be deceived into thinking they don't have seeds to sow, and that's just not true. It is also why it's critically important that we remember, remember, remember the covenant promises and blessings that God has sown on this earth throughout the ages. They are our spiritual and physical inheritance. He has declared that prosperity and wealth are seeds in themselves holding a huge amount of potential and freedom for all who believe.

Quick Truth

Remember the covenant promises and blessings that God has sown on this earth throughout the ages. They are our spiritual and physical inheritance.

Different Kinds of Seeds

The first mention of seeds in the Bible is in Genesis 1 v 11: "Then God said, 'Let the earth sprout vegetation, plants yielding seed, and trees on the earth bearing fruit according to their kind with seed in them'; and it was so." This was day three of creation, and we see that seeds are an integral part of God's creative process. God is spelling it out pretty clearly that it was Him who placed the seeds in the ground and that each herb, plant, and tree was part of a cycle of generative power. This generative principle of God's creation is a huge lesson for us to grasp when it comes to knowing, and sowing, our seeds. It is the fruit that contains more seed by being itself that is the flow of God's kingdom principles on earth. Again, we get to learn from the land. As a fun side note, it is also worth mentioning that whenever you see the word "sons" in scripture, the Hebrew root of the word is "seeds." God was the first sower of seeds and placed them all in the earth, hoping and willing the earth to bring it forth in its time.

Farmers teach us that there are two types of seeds. There is the one type of seed that when the sun hits it directly, it can do better and produce a crop. And there is another type of seed that when the sun hits it, it withers and dies and is unable to germinate. This second seed has to be planted into deeper and darker soil. My way of interpreting this is that what I sow underground, what I do in secret, no one needs to know. That's the seed that needs to go deeper and darker and more hidden. It needs that kind of condition to germinate versus the seeds sown on the surface that need light and exposure. And you know, there is testimony, grace, and abundance available for both. You just have to be paying attention to what seed needs what conditions while deeply covering it with prayer and discernment.

I want you to think about your seeds, look at your seeds, name your seeds, and sow them where you want to go! Sow where you feel called and what reflects your purpose in the kingdom of God and remember what we have been promised, as we are generous and faithful to His promises. Go back to the scriptures, look at the list of things you have inherited from others, and act accordingly. We will come back to this idea of intentionally sowing forward in the next chapter!

Dig in Your Heels – Seeds

What are the seeds in your hands?

What seeds have been sown into your life?

Where do you want to go, and where are the "fields" in your life? They could be your family, workplace, church community, the business you run, or the business you hope to grow.

Take some time to meditate on the following scriptures and let God minister to your spirit about these matters:

Matthew 13 v 1 - 43

Galatians 6 v 7

Galatians 6 v 9

Breakthrough Declarations and Decrees

Lord forgive me for any and all negligence concerning the seeds and finances you've put in my hands.

I renounce all demons of poverty that would seduce me to withhold my seeds. Lord, you give seeds to sowers. I renounce every spirit of fear that rises when an economic crisis threatens in Jesus's name.

I declare a revelation of the seeds you have planted within me from before creation. I declare their abundance, and they will germinate into an abundant crop.

Read Psalm 139 as a declaration of who you are and whose you are.

CHAPTER 9 – The Power of Sowing

"Those who work their land will have abundant food, but those who chase fantasies will have their fill of poverty."

Proverbs 28 v 19

"Remember this: Whoever sows sparingly will also reap sparingly, and whoever sows generously will also reap generously. Each of you should give what you have decided in your heart to give, not reluctantly or under compulsion, for God loves a cheerful giver. And God is able to bless you abundantly, so that in all things at all times, having all that you need, you will abound in every good work. As it is written: 'They have freely scattered their gifts to the poor; their righteousness endures forever.' "

2 Corinthians 9 v 6-9 NIV

I am really excited about this chapter, as we have already done so much work on establishing truths about prosperity, wealth, and mindset. Sowing is one of my favorite faith-fun activities, and I have seen God continually show up in small and big ways as we have sown. I believe that faith in action is to walk in the truth of prosperity when it comes to sowing targeted seeds with intentionality. So, hold on to your hats and let's dive in!

Take a moment to look over some of your notes from the prompts in this book so far. What are the common themes and motivations to your growth and prosperity? What areas of influence have you been placed in? What gets you excited?

Jesus said in Luke 6 v 38: *"Give, and it will be given to you. A good measure, pressed down, shaken together and running over, will be poured into your lap. For with the measure you use, it will be measured to you."* This is such a powerful truth! No wonder the enemy doesn't want you sowing. In fact, he would rather you have a bad case of memory loss around the whole subject. The reality of the situation is, however, that you will be the one that loses out because it goes against the natural order of God's covenantal truths. As it is promised in Genesis 8 v 22, while the earth remains, seeds, sowing, and harvest will not cease.

As I have said before, I am a textualist. I believe what I read in the Bible and I believe what Jesus taught. It is therefore inevitable that it flows through my life in every area and has the potential to create streams of living water in the areas I sow. I actually can't approach prosperity and the act of sowing in any other way. God is the source of it all, and I am so grateful that I can hold onto Him and walk this path fully with Him as my source.

Vision

Vision in motion is the spiritual kinetic energy that comes toward us as we move in the promises of God's covenantal inheritance. Simply put, it is the essence of the scripture found in James 2 *"Faith without works is dead,"* and it is extremely important. I once read that NOT to have a vision is to live someone else's, and there is also a proverb that says "Where there is no vision the people perish," so all in all, the consequences of not having a vision seem pretty debilitating. On the one hand, there is the dissatisfaction and famine of not living your unique God-given vision, and on the other hand there is a soul perishing that can happen because there simply is no vision to run toward.

Giving

God is a benevolent giver. As we walk in His covenantal promises and instructions, we are given blessings and wealth according to His riches. God's blessings make us wealthy in so many ways. They make us prosperous and as He gives to us freely and without condemnation, we learn to be the givers He always designed us to be. Remember, currency is to be in constant flow, like a river. Flowing water carries life, and consequently, stagnant water is dead. Whatever that currency is (money, time, or skills), we become less prosperous as soon as it is blocked by any scarcity mentality, dams of pride, or even greed. We lose peace, plenty, strength, and the ability to advance. Giving is a mode of sowing, and being a cheerful giver allows us to sow with a joyful anticipation of a great harvest.

Keeping giving in the forefront of our faith-filled lives is a lifestyle in itself. Giving is a lover's game (I don't mean that in sexual kind of way) and is the intimate essence of who God is. There are two statements that remind me just how much this is true: "For God so **LOVED** the world that He **GAVE** His only begotten son" (John 3 v 16). Do you see what I mean? Giving is a very deep, spiritual thing that elevates our hearts to the Father. He is a God of expansion and multiplication, and giving is the blueprint of His perfect economic plan for our growth as His kingdom workers. Just as we live in an economic world, in God's economy giving is God's method for tangible multiplication too. When we sow our seed in faith, currency flows straight from the throne of heaven to us.

Giving looks very differently for my husband and I. Giving to us means an opportunity, big or small, to be a part of an ecosystem that delivers a harvest every time. We were discussing only recently one time back when we were broke, so broke that we couldn't afford to buy chicken, when my brother-in-law was purchasing his first home and we had just been sent our tax refund. My husband wanted to help his brother with the down payment for his house and despite having very little, we gave him our whole tax refund. At that time, it was such a sacrifice to sow ALL we had to our name, but we knew that it was the kingdom thing to do in that season.

Fast forward to a couple of years later and my husband was still working for a startup company. He didn't get paid regularly and we got landed with a tax bill that we just couldn't pay for. In fact, the IRS put levies on our bank account and froze the little money we had to live on and pay our bills. My husband and I started praying; it was all we could do. I told God that I was putting a demand on heaven for my harvest on seeds that we had sown. The next morning after many attempts to get the bank to release our money, them having said no to us multiple times, I asked my husband to call the IRS and make arrangements for a payment plan. When he called the IRS, the agent told my husband, "Mr. Fernandez, your account is up-to-date; it shows that someone came into our payment processing building and paid the bill in full. The levies on your account have been lifted." He continued, "I've never seen something like this happen in all the years I've worked for the IRS. Someone came in, knew all your information, and paid your bill." We believe God sent an angel to pay for our bill using our harvest to do so!

Another example of giving that we experienced as a couple was when I was out of budget one month and needed some cash. It happened when one morning God told my husband to give me $1,000 and that I was good ground to sow. God went on to say to his spirit that He would multiply it for him if he was obedient. I will never forget that morning. Eric got up, handed me the $1,000 that I needed for the kid's party and a couple of little things I wanted to do, and was on his way to work. The very next day, my husband got a commission for $100,000. It was breathtakingly abundant and spoke of kingdom method and economy so deeply to us both.

I share these stories to say that obedience is better than sacrifice! It really is. We are so willing in our churches to sacrifice, but rarely are we willing to obey. The only reason why some of us still struggle is because someone wasn't obedient. Disobedience in sowing hinders harvest; it's as simple as that. Giving goes beyond church doors, and giving comes dressed in many different ways. However, when giving becomes a default setting, a lifestyle, you inevitably become a channel of wealth and prosperity that God can use to show the world who He is. To be a worker in His kingdom is to be a cheerful giver and to love others in the way He loves.

Tithing

Tithing is a mode of sowing, and I love how this act of obedience is talked about in the book of Malachi.

" 'Bring all the tithes into the storehouse, that there may be food in My house, and try Me now in this,' says the LORD of hosts, 'If I will not open for you the windows of heaven and pour out for you such blessing that there will not be room enough to receive it. And I will rebuke the devourer for your sakes, so that he will not destroy the fruit of your ground, nor shall the vine fail to bear fruit for you in the field,' says the LORD of hosts. 'And all nations will call you blessed. For you will be a delightful land,' says the LORD of hosts."

Malachi 3 v 10-12

When we tithe, we open the windows of heaven and keep that currency of the kingdom of God in full motion. Tithing is part of the cycle, the flow, and God promises to protect and grow all that we tithe for the grace and glory of His kingdom.

Thus, it's more than an obligation but a privilege to sow the part of my seed that is not meant for consumption.

What do I mean by that, you ask? Well, have you ever bitten into any fruit that is sweet and juicy but if you bite into the seed it's bitter?! That's what I mean by not meant for consumption. You can eat and enjoy the whole fruit except for the few seeds in it—those are to be sown. That's the reason why they aren't pleasant to your tastes, but it's what keeps the harvest of multiple fruits coming. Without seeds sown, there is no harvest. Tithing is a method of covenant relationship that is meant to be done in faith with a cheerful heart, moving in holy expectation.

Trusting and Honoring

As I said at the beginning of this book, I take God radically at His word, and because of this it is easy to trust Him with everything! Trust is about, in one sense, giving God complete power of attorney, trusting that He will work on my behalf and for my best interest and for the prosperity of me and my family. To commune with God in this way is strengthening and can feel vulnerable all at the same time, but I have committed to being of one sound mind when it comes to trust, and God has never let me down.

As we sow the seeds placed within us and in our hands, we learn to honor God with our wealth, our time, and our skills. There are so many ways to honor God. In worship and good works, for example, but another way that we honor God is with substance! Honor looks like something, and others witness that honoring. Part of the way I honor God with the seeds of financial prosperity in my life is to tell others about it. This isn't for the purpose of bragging but for the purpose of honor. As I share and testify to the seeds that I sow—the ones that need exposure and light, that is—I have seen other people's faith grow too. Honoring means to give weight to something, and all honor and glory goes to God for seeds of faith that He has sown in my life ever since I was a child.

"Honor thy Lord with your wealth, and with the first fruits of all thine increase: So shall thy barns be filled with plenty, and thy presses shall burst out with new wine."

Proverbs 3 v 9-10

The joy available to us when we sow the seeds of kingdom purpose can't be matched with anything. We have the privilege and calling on our lives to be kingdom sowers. Jesus is our greatest example of what it means to be a sower of covenantal promises and living in the birthright of our kingdom inheritance.

Quick Truth

Vision in motion is the spiritual kinetic energy that comes toward us as we move in the promises of God's covenantal inheritance.

Dig in Your Heels

VISION

A vision statement is the ideal scenario declared over your future and is one of the anchors in our lives when the mission feels heavy and our faith feels a little battered. It is written down and placed somewhere you can read it regularly. It is also written in present tense despite being a statement of the future. What will your vision statement be? This is a "With God, anything is possible" moment. So, do some freewriting in your journal. I'm excited for the things that God envisions within you with your prosperity mindset in full action.

SOWING

With your vision in mind, where have you been sowing? Is this aligned with your vision?

Where would you like to sow intentionally, and what are you asking God?

Where have you sowed?

Breakthrough Declarations and Decrees – Sowing

Lord, as I practice sowing, tithing, giving offerings, alms, first fruits, and sacrificial giving, I ask you to judge and render ineffective every function of poverty assigned to shut me out of increase and abundance in the name of Jesus.

Every assignment of hand-to-mouth and week-to-week living because of poverty, financial ignorance, and poor stewardship is broken in Jesus's name!

I ask your forgiveness for every time I've turned a deaf ear toward the needy and refused to help those who you've empowered me to bless.

"Whoever pursues righteousness and love finds life, prosperity, and honor." (Psalm 21 v 21)

I decree and declare that my health will be in full alignment with your purposes and plans. I declare that as I sow into my health and healing journey, you will place before me all I need when it comes to my physical well-being and overall health.

CHAPTER 10 – The Power of Holy Expectation

"For the creation waits in eager expectation for the children of God to be revealed."

Romans 8 v 19

"In the morning, Lord, you hear my voice. In the morning I lay my requests before you and wait expectantly."

Psalm 5 v 3

"Now He who supplies the seed to the sower and bread for food will also supply and increase your store of seed and will enlarge the harvest of your righteousness."

2 Corinthians 9 v 10

You have to anticipate your harvest, which means you have to get your hopes up. You have to "sell" your fruit before it is ready and prepare for the harvest season! This is what it means to have a holy expectation and to trust the process of the seeds. It is also an integral part of honoring God's hand of grace on your life and the work of your hands too. We get to wait in holy expectation as the Holy Spirit has guided, guarded, and led each act of trust. It has to be a holy work, a work set apart while still getting your hands dirty and in the earth. Sowing has order to it, but the scattering of seeds can sometimes look messy and chaotic.

Bringing a harvest in is a season of great celebration, and the scriptures show us a cycle designed by God to celebrate biblical holidays in line with the agricultural calendar. There is great reward for sowing, watering, protecting, and nurturing the seeds to full term. Seeing the abundance of the harvest symbolizes a season dedicated to a lot of hard work and sacrifice. When it comes to a spiritual harvest, our expectations can be the same. The order is the same, after all, and the prayer and purpose of the spiritual seeds we sow will have to go through a similar process. We sow, we wait, and we reap, and we have to pay attention to nurturing those seeds and watering them with prayer and declaration. The only thing about spiritual seeds is that the time between the sowing and the reaping can be a longer season than we expect.

There is a conversation about how and where the seeds get scattered that Jesus teaches in Matthew 13. This parable teaches us a very practical approach to sowing with more intentionality. Take a moment to read Matthew 13 v 1-23. I believe that we have to be aware of what eyes we see with when it comes to spiritual seeds and harvest. My prayer is always that God will give me eyes to see His harvest, to see where the enemy has come in like a crow and stolen seeds, and also to see where seed has been sown in unhealthy places. There is a lot of faith and discernment needed to see the economy of His kingdom in real time and learn how to see as He sees.

The Season of Harvest

Are you due for a harvest? Maybe you are struggling to see the return in your life and find yourself in a time of waiting and watching while your crops grow and your trees come to a place of fruitfulness. A harvest in your individual and family life will look different than a communal harvest, but as the scriptures tell us, all things work together for those walking in covenant promise with God.

There is no disconnection in my head when it comes to my lived experience and the promises of God. Yes, there is process and things to learn, which can often mean moments of discomfort, suffering, and challenge, but the ultimate truth is that God is a God of blessing. There are also a few things that I live by if you want to see a visible return in your life when it comes to harvesting.

Play Your Part

If you sow it, you have to be prepared to harvest it. You have to become almost aggressive about harvesting and not forget about your crop. Otherwise, it will rot in the field, and the enemy will find ways to make use of it too. God won't do the reaping for us, just like He won't do the sowing. We have to be willing to work the field of our lives and be dedicated to the cycle.

Don't Give Up

I love the scripture found in Galatians 6 v 9: "So let's not get tired of doing what is good. At just the right time, we will reap a harvest of blessing if we don't give up." Yes, there is a season of waiting, but the key is what we do in that time of waiting. Part of the waiting is learning to declare with your words a holy expectation over the harvest that will come.

Weeds

We are fully in the process when we start talking about weeds. We are in the field, surveying our crop, and sometimes weeds can creep into the field. This is about protecting your crop and not just leaving the field to get on with it. Weeds can look like unforgiveness, bitterness, and walking outside of love. The best way to keep the weeds at bay is to keep watch over your heart/mind and pull them up from the root when you see them crop up. You can also spray them with the word and Spirit.

Work and Guard

In Genesis 2 v 15, God places man in the garden to "work and guard" it, but the English translation here doesn't really do the instruction justice. The roots of these words in the Hebrew give us even more insight into how God's kingdom works. The word "work" in biblical Hebrew is the word *"avodah,"* which has five root meanings. These are to work, to worship, to serve, servant, and slave. So this is the first time we see the word "worship" in scripture too. This is a huge biblical concept that starts in the garden of Eden and is partnered here with the word "guard," which is sometimes translated in English as "keep." The root of this word is "to hear." Therefore, when it comes to holy expectation and harvest, we can set our hearts to worship in the hearing and work at building God's kingdom on earth as it was originally designed. To have a kingdom mindset is to work and guard the garden on earth as it is in heaven.

Don't Forget to Water

The ecosystem of the places we sow need watering in practical ways. To neglect the seed would mean the crop would be lost. I love *The Message* translation of Psalm 65. It is so poetic and gives a real picture of the beauty of harvest.

> *"Oh, visit the earth, ask her to join the dance!*
> *Deck her out in spring showers, fill the God-River with*
> *living water.*
> *Paint the wheat fields golden.*
> *Creation was made for this!*
> *Drench the plowed fields, soak the dirt clods with rainfall*
> *as harrow and rake bring her to blossom and fruit."*

Psalm 65 v 9

Praise and thanksgiving are the language of faith and harvest. We sow our seeds and nurture them with praise that waters them with holy expectation.

Be Ready with Your Tools for Harvest

When the crops look ready, a farmer has a tool to measure the moisture of the crop. The moisture content of the crop has to be within certain parameters so it doesn't spoil once it is in the storehouse. They have a little tool that measures this moisture level and once the reading displays perfect conditions for harvesting, they have a tiny window to get the crop in. The scriptures even give us a hint to how important timing is. In Mark 4 v 29, it says, *"But when the grain is ripe and permits, immediately he sends forth the reapers and puts in the sickle, because the harvest stands ready."*

The second most important tool is that of the sickle. This instrument is very sharp and has been used for cutting crops for centuries. Of course, there are huge machines that do this now in many places, but the principle is the same. At the time of harvest, our tools of faith must be sharp and ready. Again, I see God's word playing a huge role in the harvest, as it says in Hebrews 4 v 12, *"For the Word of God is alive and powerful. It is sharper than the sharpest two-edged sword . . ."* I love this picture of how the words of our sowing and the words of our harvest are critically important to the whole process.

Cry Out

Again, this is a cry of faith. It is not begging but a command for the harvest to come forth. When the harvest is ready, it will make itself known to its rightful owner and our job is to be paying attention, listening, and watching for the harvests in our lives.

As I said at the beginning of this chapter, holy expectation is about Jesus, our living hope guiding, guarding, and causing us to see as He sees for when the harvest is ready and what is required of us in the waiting.

Dig in Your Heels – Holy Expectation

I have drawn together a few declarations and decrees for you to use as prompts below. However, now is the time to dig in your heels and write your own decrees and declarations. You have done so much work on the subject of prosperity and covenantal growth, and you have all you need to write from your new mindset holy expectations over your process of sowing and harvest.

Breakthrough Declarations and Decrees

I renounce the seed waster, seed eater, and seed destroyer that works against my income, increase, and harvest in Jesus's name . . . GO!!!

I am not just a good sower and a good giver. I am a good reaper too. I am created to bring in the harvest.

I am expecting an abundant harvest. I am expecting a record-breaking harvest.

"Let them shout for joy and rejoice, who favor my vindication; and let them say continually, 'The Lord be magnified, who delights in the prosperity of His servant.' " Psalm 35 v 27

"Oh, visit the earth, ask her to join the dance! Deck her out in spring showers, fill the God-River with living water. Paint the wheat fields golden. Creation was made for this! Drench the plowed fields, soak the dirt clods with rainfall as harrow and rake bring her to blossom and fruit." Psalm 65 v 9

CONCLUSION – Prosperity Is NOT Luck, It's Your Birthright

"The Spirit of the Lord is on me, because he has anointed me to proclaim good news to the poor.
He has sent me to proclaim freedom for the prisoners and recovery of sight for the blind, to set the oppressed free, to proclaim the year of the Lord's favor."

Luke 4 v 18 / Isaiah 61

"But remember the Lord your God, for it is He who gives you the ability to produce wealth, and so confirms His covenant, which He swore to your ancestors, as it is today."

Deuteronomy 8 v 18

"I am the vine; you are the branches. If you remain in me and I in you, you will bear much fruit; apart from me, you can do nothing."

John 15 v 5

The Power of Prosperity and Covenantal Revelation

Do you get it now? That prosperity is not luck but a birthright. I really hope so, because there is such an abundance of life waiting for us all as we live in obedience with His word and promises. To me, living in and from the foundations of these promises are what it means to love God, to love each other, and to even love the stranger. Living the cycle of prosperity (seed, sowing, reaping, and harvest) is the proclamation of good news to the poor. It is a proclamation of freedom for the prisoners. It is a recovery of sight that links us right back to the beginning of Abraham's calling from God too. Can you see it? Do you remember what God said in Genesis 12? God says to Abraham that he would go to a land that God would cause him to see, a land of generative blessings where the oppression of scarcity and fear-based mindsets have to stop. It is a declaration that a new season will rise up, an eternal year of the Lord's favor!

The guts and grace of it all is that prosperity in our lives is possible and personal because of the presence of God weaving His way throughout our whole story. A prosperous life comes from God and He puts a generative power inside each one of us to be generous givers from the living currency of His kingdom. A living water, indeed! We are empowered and have been entrusted with much first and foremost because God is God, and second because He is the greatest storyteller. His ways are higher than ours, and it is because of the promises made to Abraham that we all get to stand here in faith today.

Words, Mindset, and Source

Jesus is our greatest example of living a life completely inside the heart/mind of God. His words directly address the conditions of the people with grace, wisdom, and boldness. He taught in parables so that people would have a flying chance of remembering His teachings while motivating the crowds, and the few, to implement them in their everyday lives. He challenged mindsets and was always drawing people back to the teachings of Moses and the Fathers of His faith, and it is with this faith that we boldly choose to pursue His kingdom on earth.

Come on now, friends, how tempting is it just to stick all our needs on credit? How enticing is that new car smell and that seemingly good rate of repayments? I've been there! But don't forget that this whole conversation of prosperity has to be rooted in believing what God has said, and well, He doesn't run on a credit card economy. God is the source of it all and is a holy economy by being Himself! God will provide all your needs according to His glorious riches. He works on an eternal scale with unlimited resources. All He asks is that we remember He is the source of it all and that we can ask for what we want as well as what we need. As long as our motivations are rooted in seeing His kingdom come on earth, it's all good. To God be the glory. Amen.

God's Kingdom

All our spiritual and physical wealth comes from God. He gives us the power to generate wealth in small and big ways, and as we do what comes naturally, with intentionality, we have the joy of really experiencing our life on this earth in a new way. The seeds in our lives can be our time, effort, and financial resources.

"Then you say in your heart, 'My power and the might of my hand have gained me this wealth.' And you shall remember the LORD your God, for it is He who gives you power to get wealth . . ."

Deuteronomy 8 v 17-18

Recognizing that wealth is gained through the power of God, the life of Jesus, and the faith-building strength of the Holy Spirit reminds us that it is not our power that makes wealth happen. We must remain humble, and in doing so the doors of heaven open to bless the work of our hands and, well, the camel will be able to pass through the Eye of the Needle. When we leave God out of the equation, it limits the potential of your seeds. You see, God can't multiply it unless you believe that ultimately it comes from Him. Just as Jesus taught about the rich young ruler and how wealth is not kingdom prosperity, so I have learned that anything that I have loaded my life with that isn't part of His covenantal inheritance has had to be removed. If I don't, I literally can't function in my calling or see the seeds I am to sow. The power of God's presence really does have to become the quiet whisper of direction every step of the way. There has been so much beauty in experiencing God trust me with what He has bestowed in my life.

Remember, the seeds of our lives are anything that you give for purpose on purpose and sometimes even unconsciously just by being who you are. Seeds could be time, money, hope, resources, faith, love—the list is endless, really. They could also be seeds of encouragement, the seeds that are a sign that tells the person, organization, or business that you believe in them and that you see them. The seed of trust and the seed of joy—all these seeds that have the potential to bring forth life and a harvest that will feed those around you, including the next generation. The seeds of our lives are prayers of our lives. They are a beautiful way of communicating with God and with each other and are what make us closer.

Sowing and Holy Expectation

The kingdom of God is a method on earth as it is in heaven. I no longer find myself waiting for something that can be embraced in faith NOW. Each tiny seed in my hand, my heart, my actions, and my words gets to be sown on the earth with a holy expectation.

I have experienced over and over again the smile of God when I have been able to afford a car I have asked for or a vacation that has been longed for with friends or family. As I have sowed seeds, I have asked for the abundance of the harvest to come and have declared and trusted that the fruit would be abundant. God has had me and my family in seasons and cycles like the rest of humanity, but this I know: I have always come to see the goodness of God in the land of the living, and I know I will continue to.

In our giving, tithing, and trusting God, we can wait with holy expectation. As God wakes us up to our birthright as believers, we can be transformed by the renewing of our minds and then everything can flow from a place of prosperity. We are to play our part by being prepared, not giving up, tending the fields of our lives, pulling up weeds, and guarding the boundaries so the enemy can't get in to destroy the harvest. We must grab the tools, water the crops, and declare a rich and bountiful harvest. We can cry out in holy expectation that God will be God whenever the harvest is ready, and we, too, will be prepared and ready to bring it to the storehouses of His kingdom on earth.

A Final Note

I hope you have been convinced that prosperity is far beyond a lucky hand and is a fundamental part of the Christian faith. I hope you have been encouraged to keep on digging into this subject of prosperity and that your testimonies of faith will inspire the next generation. After all, that is the point: to teach our kids in the way they should go, to teach them how to listen for the voice of God in their lives, and to live in their God-ordained birthright of prosperity here on earth.

Now, dig your heels in and go live the prosperous life that has always been available to you.

Love, Ruth

Made in United States
North Haven, CT
29 July 2022